PIANO | VOCAL | GUITAR ■ CD   **VOLUME 82**

LIONEL RICHIE

Cover photo © Alan Silfen

ISBN 978-1-4234-3431-3

7777 W. BLUEMOUND RD. P.O. BOX 13819 MILWAUKEE, WI 53213

Visit Hal Leonard Online at
www.halleonard.com

CONTENTS

ALL NIGHT LONG
(All Night)

Words and Music by
LIONEL RICHIE

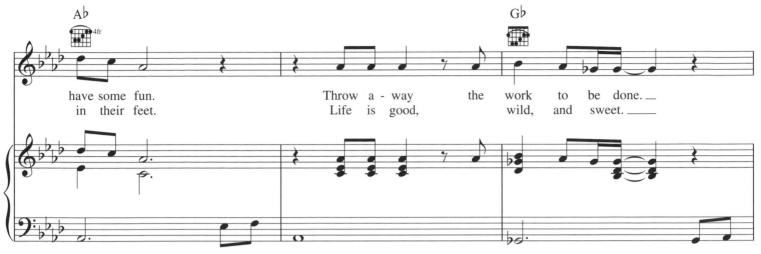

have some fun.
in their feet.

Throw a - way the work to be done.____
Life is good, wild, and sweet.____

Let the mu - sic play on. (Play on, play on.)   Ev - 'ry - bod - y sing,____
Let the mu - sic play on. (Play on, play on.)   Feel it in your heart

____ ev - 'ry - bod - y dance.   Lose your-self in wild ro - mance.   We're going to
and feel it in your soul.   Let the mu - sic take con - trol.   We're going to

par - ti' ka - ra - mu,   *fi - es - ta,*   for-ev - er.   Come on ___ and
par - ti' lim - ing,   *fi - es - ta,*   for-ev - er.   Come on ___ and

Play 1st time only

sing a - long.___ We're going___ to par - ty, ka - ra - mu, fi - es - ta, for - ev - er.

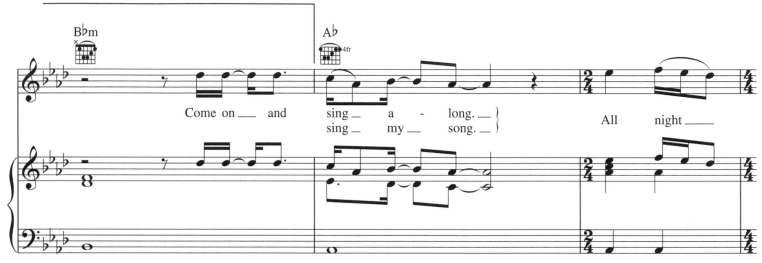

Come on___ and sing___ a - long.___ / sing___ my___ song.___ } All night___

long, ___ all night.___ All night long, ___ all night. _

___ All night ___ long, all night.___ All night _

long. _____   Ev -'ry - one ___ you meet, _   they're

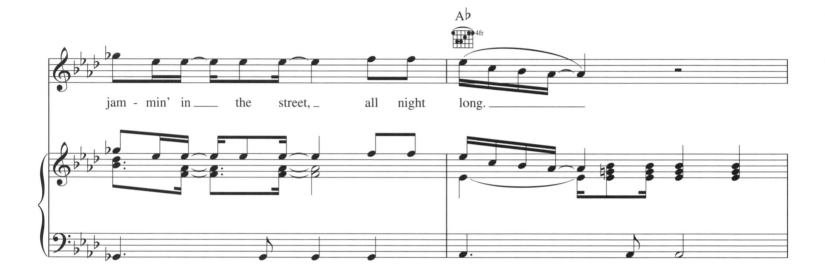

jam - min' in ___ the   street, _   all night   long. _____

SAY YOU, SAY ME

from the Motion Picture WHITE NIGHTS

Words and Music by
LIONEL RICHIE

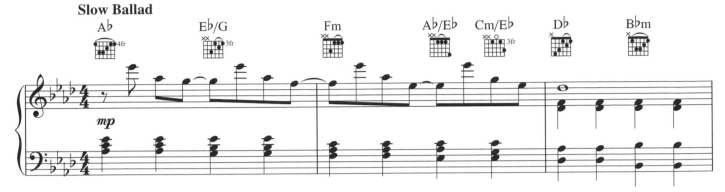

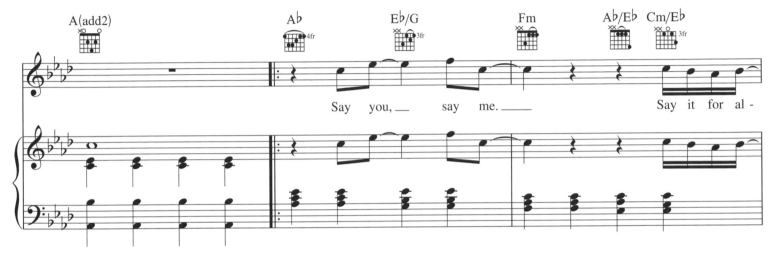

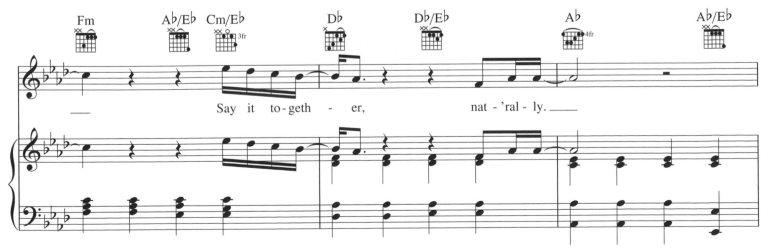

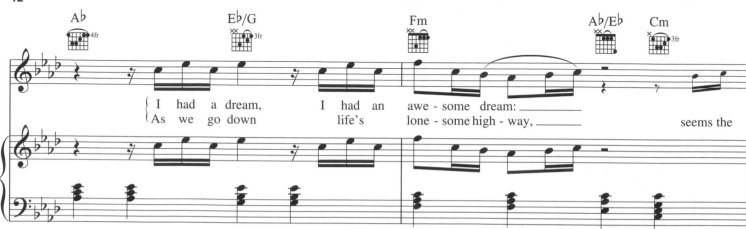

I had a dream, I had an awe-some dream:_____
As we go down life's lone-some high-way,_____ seems the

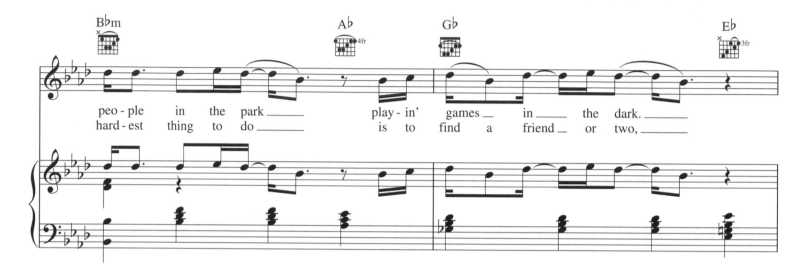

peo-ple in the park _____ play-in' games __ in ____ the dark. _____
hard-est thing to do _____ is to find a friend __ or two, _____

And what they played was a mas-quer-ade. _____ But from be -
that help-ing hand, some-one who un - der - stands. _____ And when you

hind the walls __ of doubt, ____ a voice was cry - ing out. _____
feel you've lost ____ your way, ____ you've got

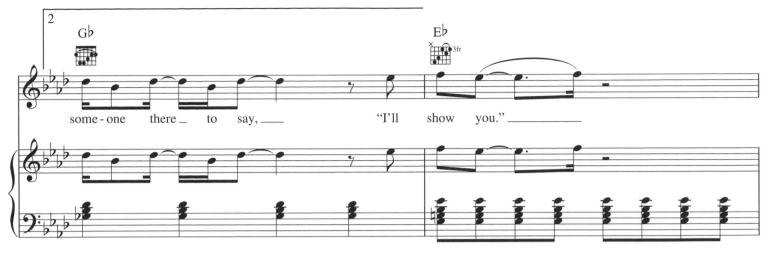

some-one there __ to say, ___ "I'll show you." ____

Say you, ___ say me. ____ Say it for al-

-ways. That's the way it should be. ____

Say you, ___ say me. ____ Say it to-geth-

Faster

-er, nat - 'ral - ly. _____ So you

think you know _____ the an - swers. Oh, _____ no. _____ Well, the

whole world's got ya danc - in', that's right, I'm _____ tell - in' you. It's

time to start _____ be - liev - in', oh, _____ yes. _____ Be -

Tempo I

lieve in who — you are; ____ you are a shin - ing star. ____

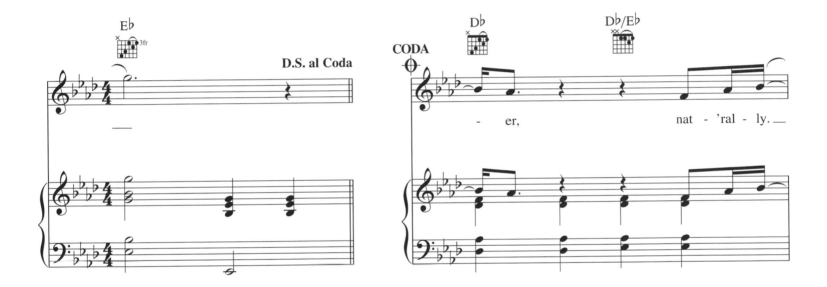

D.S. al Coda

____

CODA

- er, nat - 'ral - ly. __

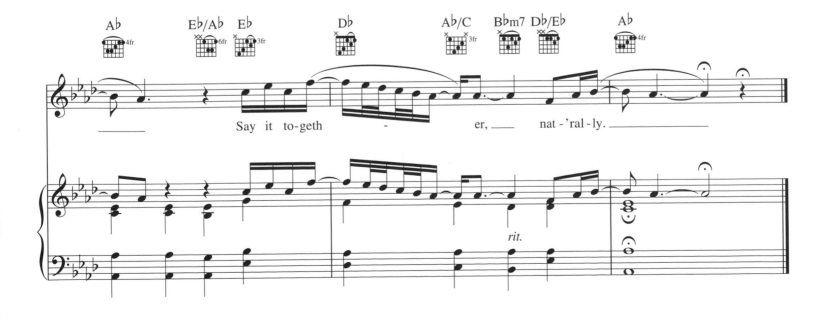

Say it to-geth - er, ____ nat -'ral -ly. ____

rit.

LADY

Words and Music by
LIONEL RICHIE

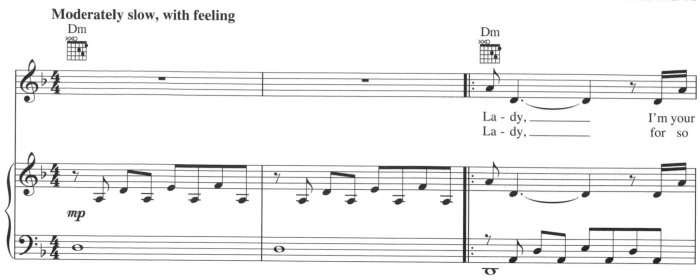

Moderately slow, with feeling

La - dy, _____ I'm your
La - dy, _____ for so

knight in shin - ing ar - mor and I love you, _____ you have made me what I
man - y years I thought I'd nev - er find you, _____ you have come in - to my

am and _____ I am yours. _____
life and _____ made me whole. _____
For -

My love, _____ there's so man-y ways I want to say I love you, _____ let me
ev - er, _____ let me wake to see you each and ev-'ry morn-ing, _____ let me

hold _ you in my arms for - ev - er - more. _____
hear _ you whis-per soft-ly _____ in my ear. _____

You have gone _____ and made me such a fool, _
In my eyes _____ I see no one else but you, _

I'm _ so lost in your love. And oh, we be-
there's no oth-er love like our love. And yes, oh yes, I'll

long   to-geth-er,   won't you be-lieve __ in my   song? _____

al-ways want you near me,   I've wait-ed for you __ for so   long. _____

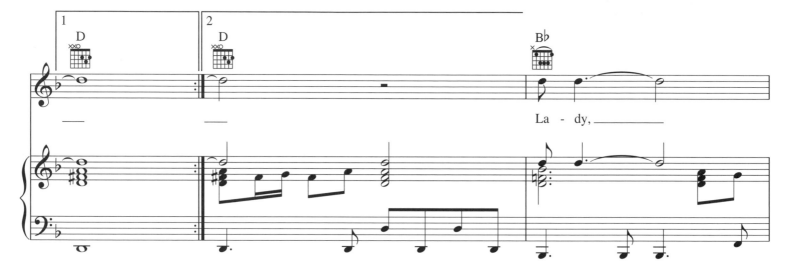

La - dy, _____

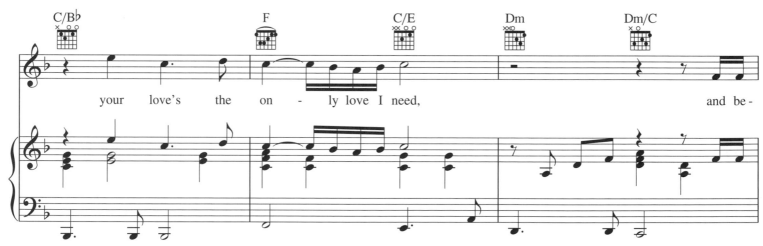

your   love's   the   on - ly   love   I   need,   and be-

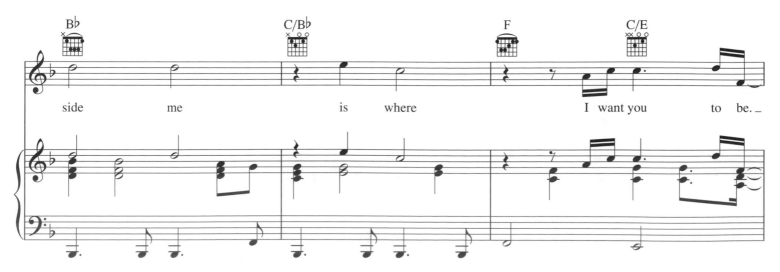

side   me   is   where   I want you   to   be. __

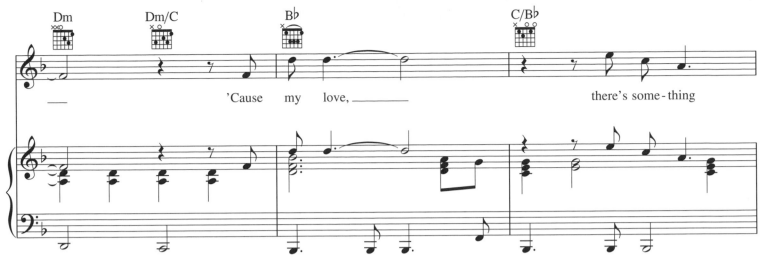

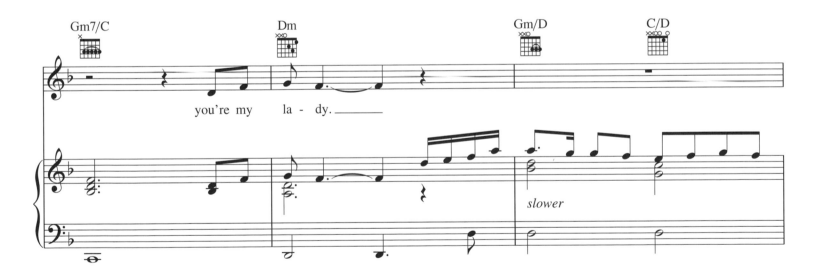

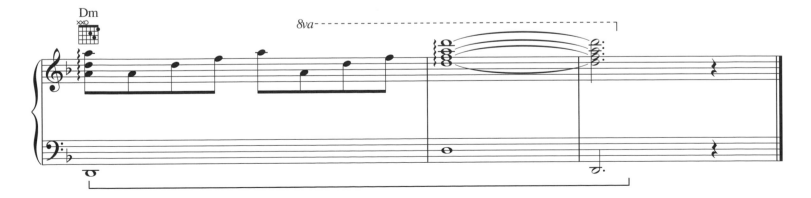

PENNY LOVER

Words and Music by LIONEL RICHIE
and BRENDA HARVEY-RICHIE

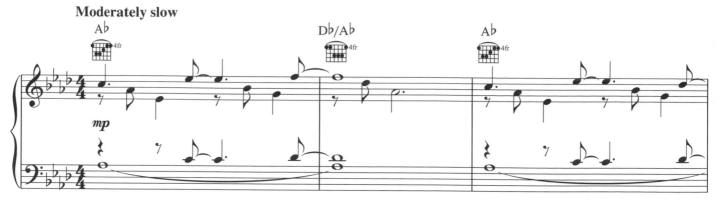

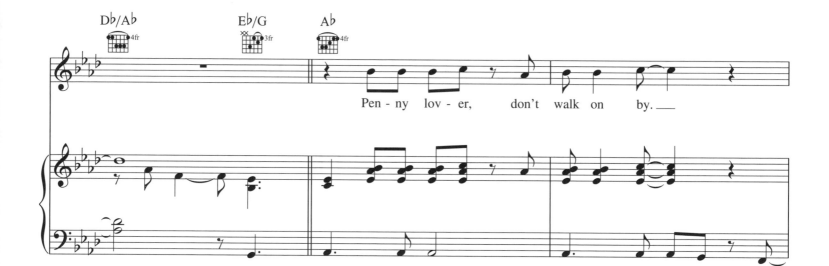

Pen - ny lov - er, don't walk on by. ___

Pen - ny lov - er, don't you make me cry. ___   Can't you see, girl, who my

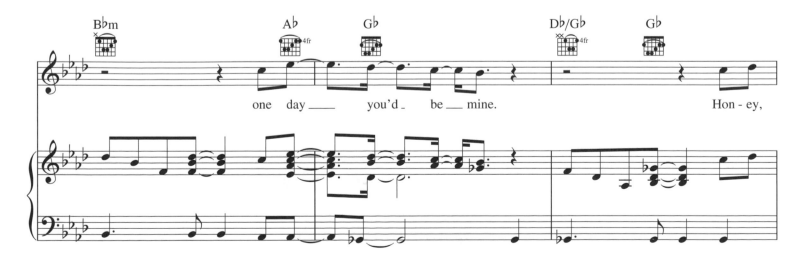

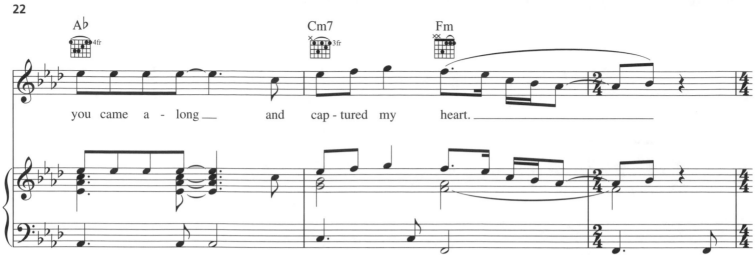

you came a - long ___ and cap - tured my heart. _____

Now my love is some-where lost ___ in your ___ kiss. When I'm

all a - lone ___ it's you that I miss. Girl, a love like yours is hard ___ to re-

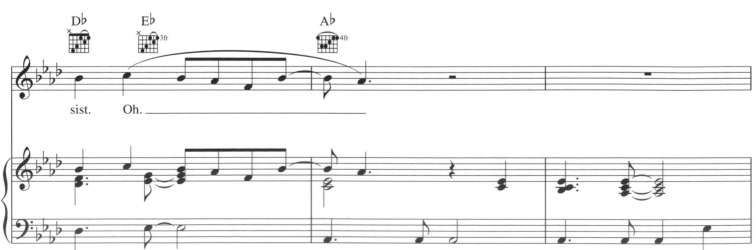

sist. Oh. _____

Girl, __ I sur - ren - der. What more __

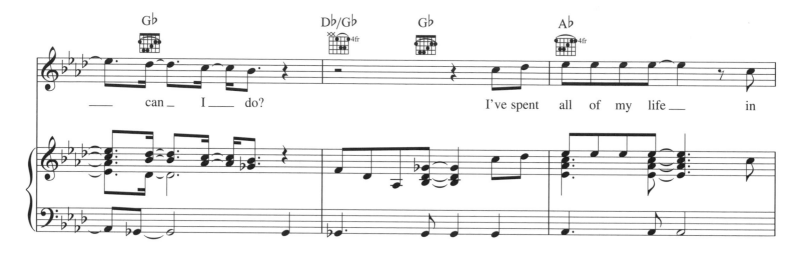

__ can __ I __ do? I've spent all of my life __ in

search of your love. __ Now there's

one more thing I'd __ like to say: Don't you ev - er take your sweet __ love a -

way. Girl, I'll do _____ an-y-thing, just please stay. Oh. _____

_____ I don't un-der-stand

it, oh, _____ what's come o - ver me. _____

But I'm _ not _ gon-na wor - ry, no, _ not an-y - more, _____

'cause when a man's ___ in love ___ he's on - ly got one sto -

- ry. That's why my love is some-where lost ___ in your ___

___ kiss. When I'm lost and a - lone ___ it's you

that I miss. With a love like yours, it's hard to re - sist. Oh, _____ oh. _

Pen - ny lov - er, don't

walk on by. ___ (Don't you walk ___ on ___ by.) Pen - ny lov - er, don't you

make me cry. ___ (Don't you make ___ me cry, ba - by.) Pen - ny lov - er, don't

walk on by. ___ (Don't you walk ___ on ___ by.) Pen - ny lov - er, don't you

28

STILL

Words and Music by
LIONEL RICHIE

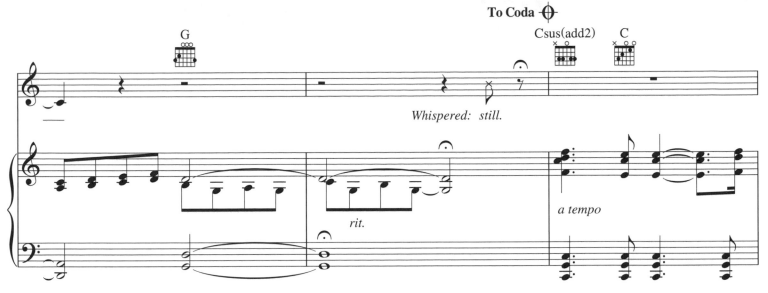

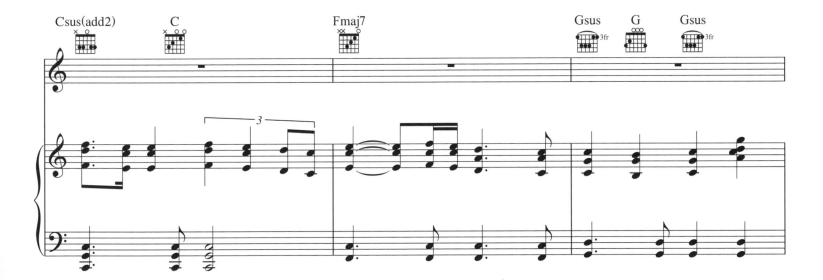

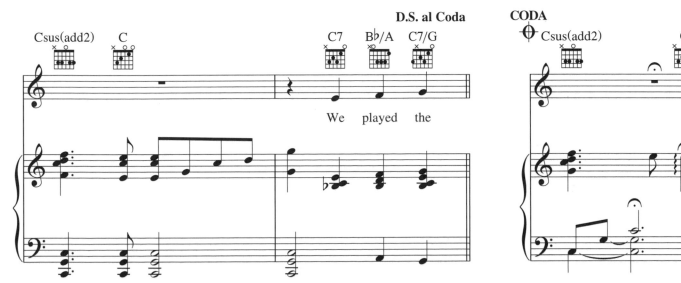

THREE TIMES A LADY

Words and Music by
LIONEL RICHIE

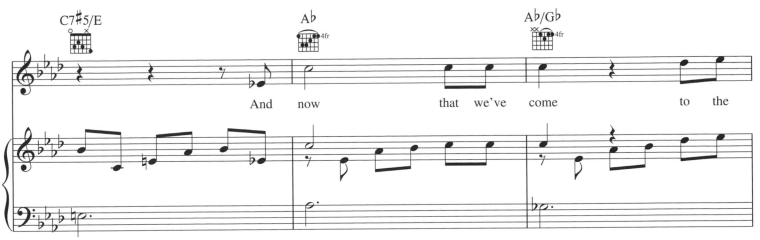

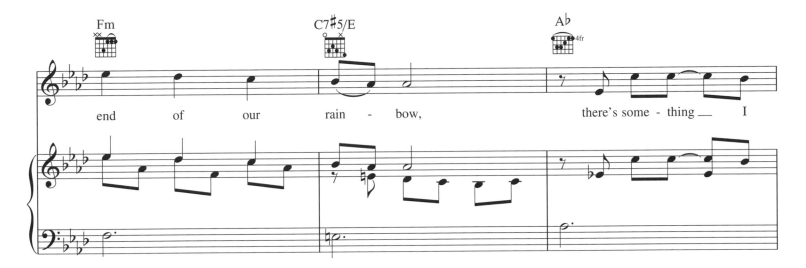

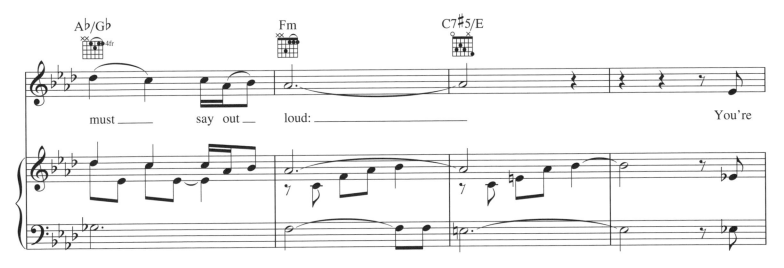

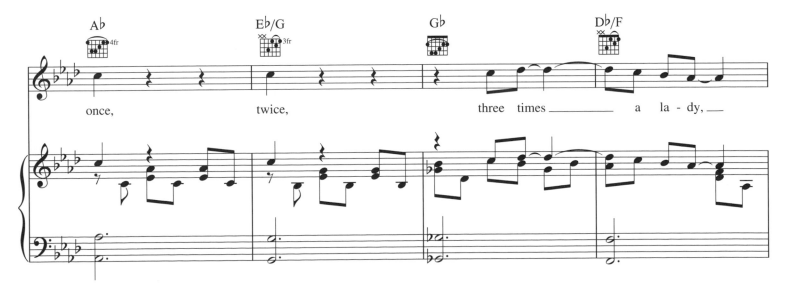

36

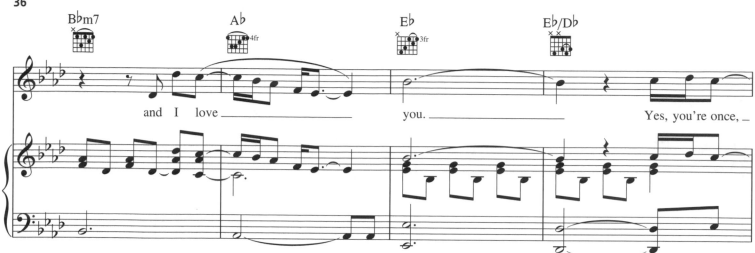

and I love _____ you. _____ Yes, you're once, _

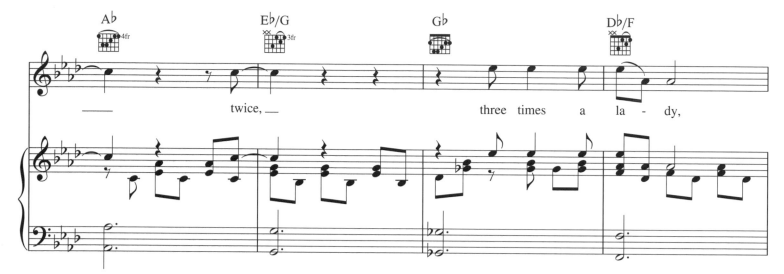

_ twice, _ three times a la-dy,

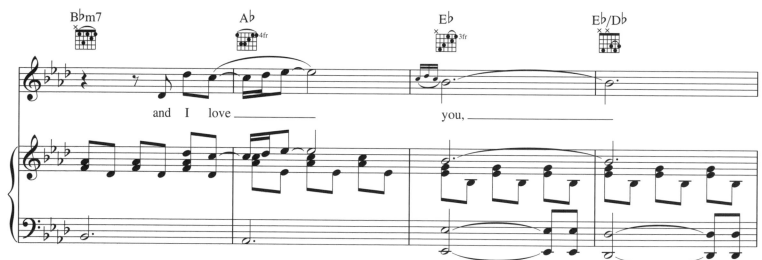

and I love _____ you, _____

I love _____ you. _____

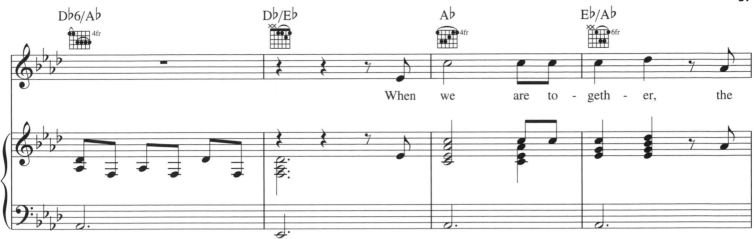

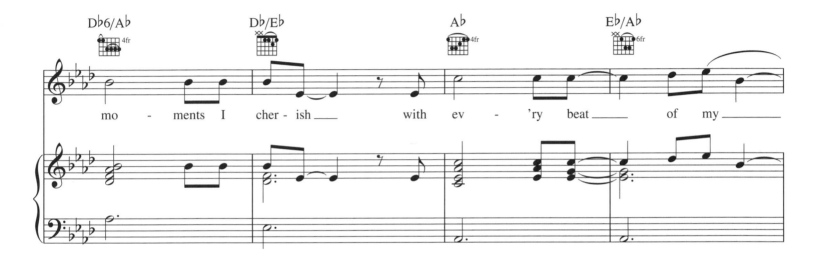

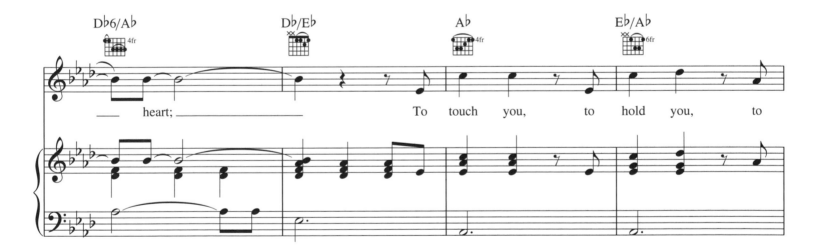

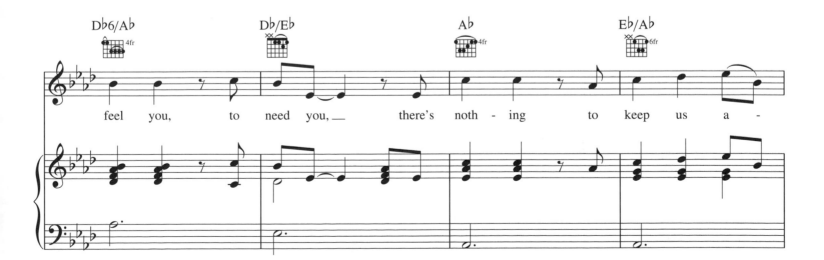

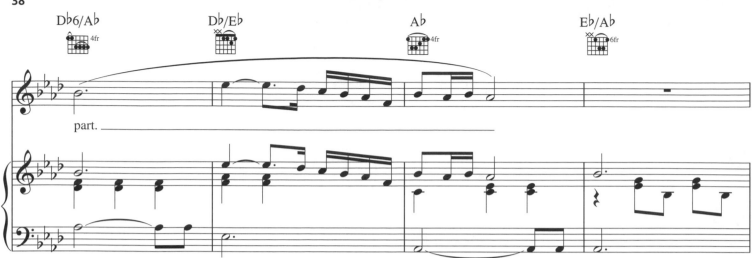

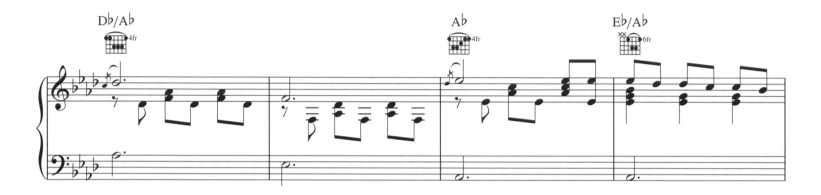

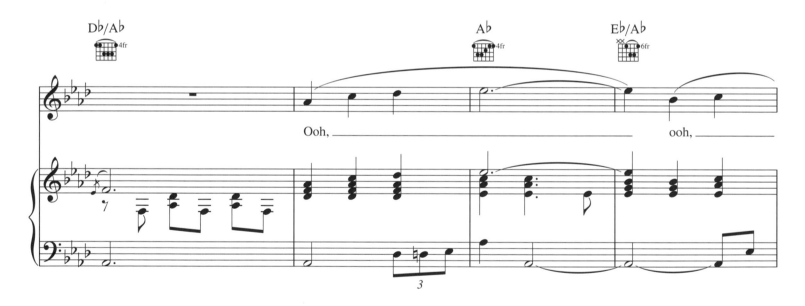

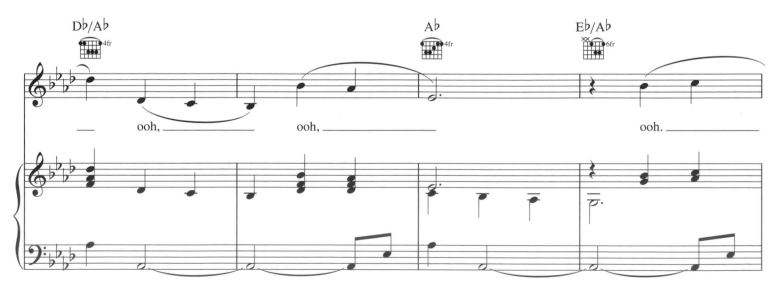

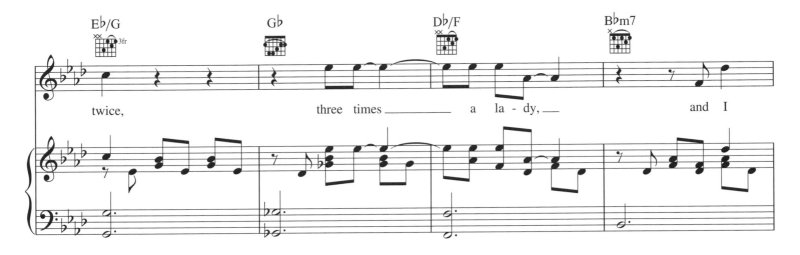

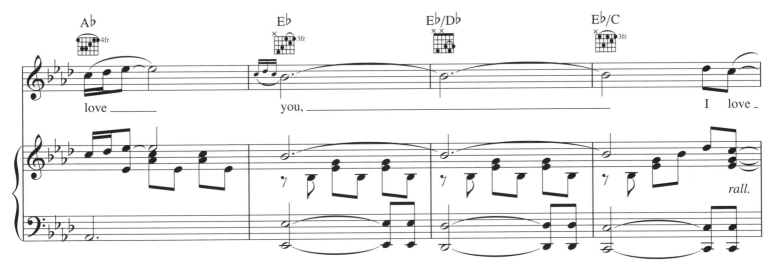

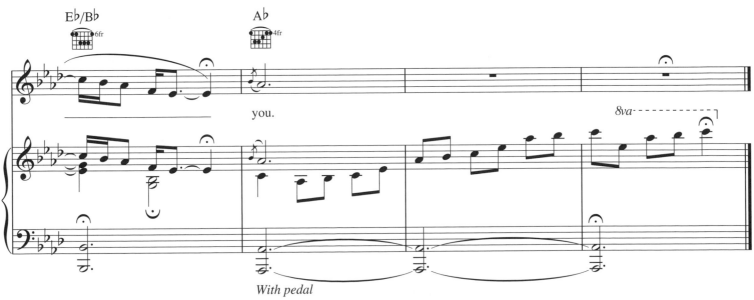

TRULY

Words and Music by
LIONEL RICHIE

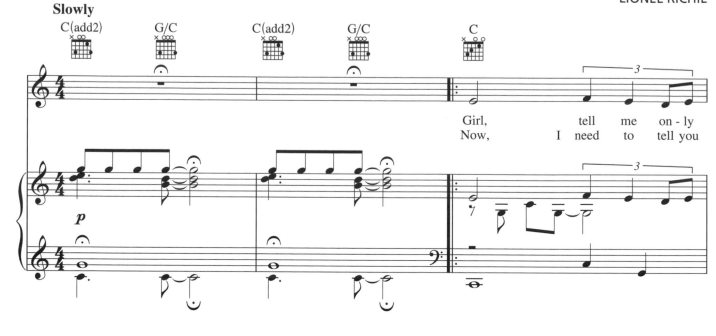

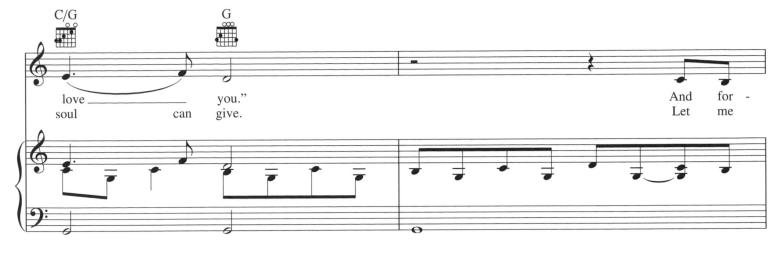

love ____ you." And for -
soul can give. Let me

ev - er, ____ I will be your
hold you. ____ I need to have you

lov - er, ____ and I know if
near me, ____ and I feel, with

you ____ real - ly care
you ____ in my   I will
                        arms, this

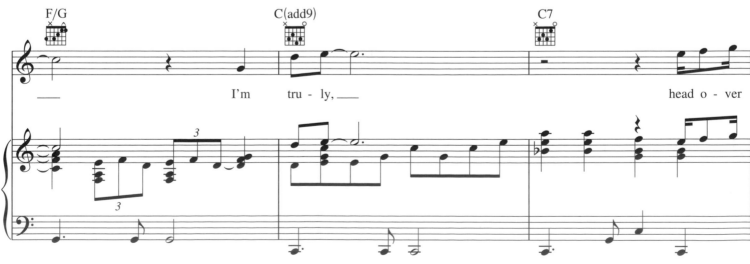

STUCK ON YOU

Words and Music by
LIONEL RICHIE

Moderate Country

(1.,3.) Stuck on   you, ___   I've got this   feel - in' down   deep in my soul ___
(2.) Stuck on   you, ___   been a   fool too ___   long, I guess it's

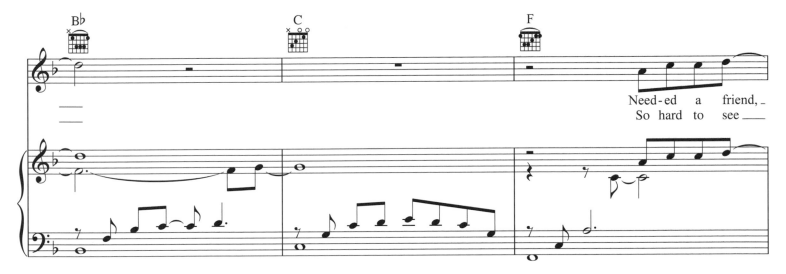

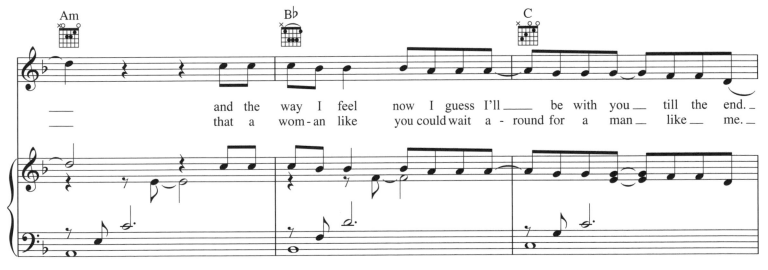

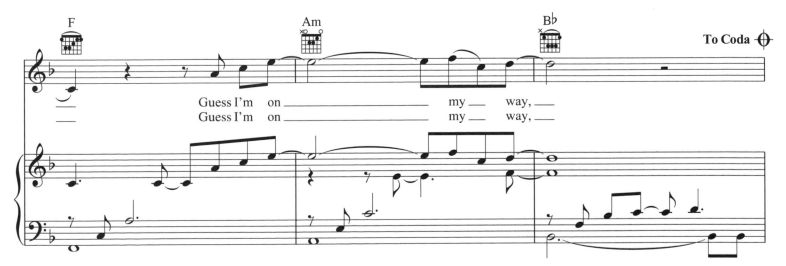

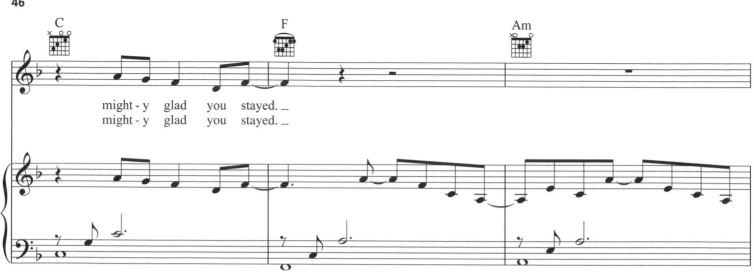

might - y glad you stayed. _
might - y glad you stayed. _

Oh, I'm leav - ing on ____ that mid - night train to - mor -

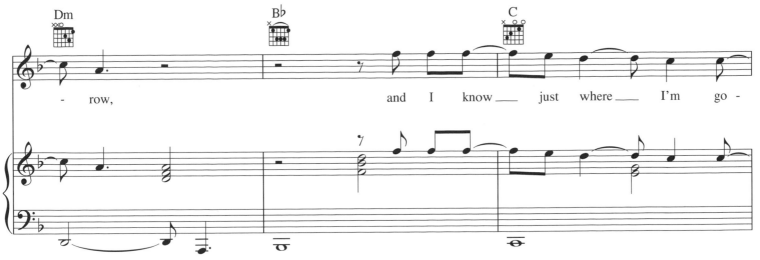

-row, and I know ___ just where ___ I'm go-

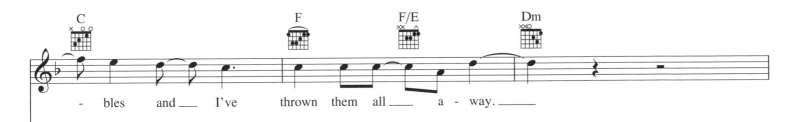

-in'. ___ I've packed up my trou-

-bles and ___ I've thrown them all ___ a- way. ___

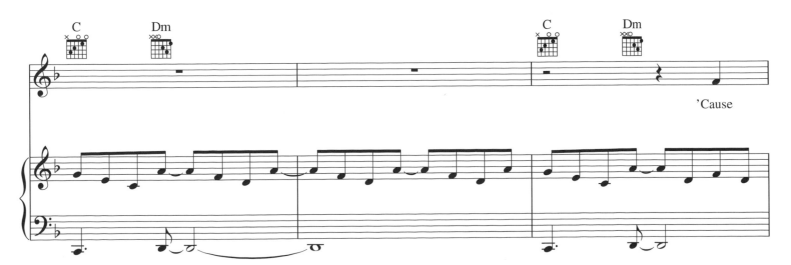

'Cause

this time, lit - tle dar - lin', I'm com - in' home ___ to

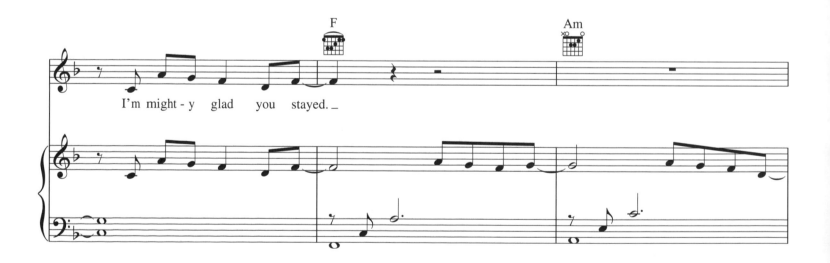

D.S. al Coda

stay, ___ ah.

CODA

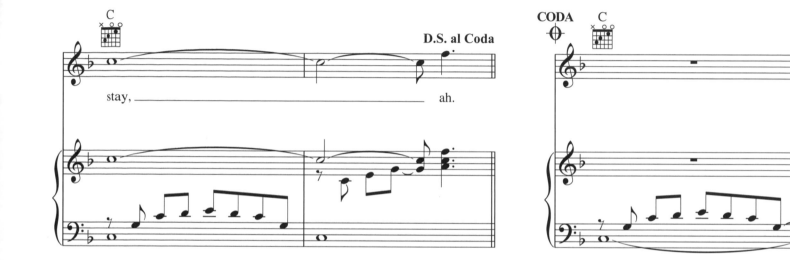

I'm might - y glad you stayed. _

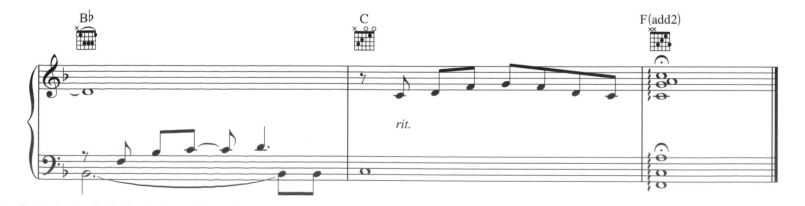

rit.